Music by
RICHARD RODGERS

Lyrics by
LORENZ HART

ISBN 978-0-634-06610-8

WILLIAMSON MUSIC®
A RODGERS AND HAMMERSTEIN COMPANY
www.williamsonmusic.com

EXCLUSIVELY DISTRIBUTED BY

HAL•LEONARD®
CORPORATION
7777 W. BLUEMOUND RD. P.O. BOX 13819 MILWAUKEE, WI 53213

Visit Hal Leonard Online at
www.halleonard.com

YOUR *PAL JOEY*

By Bert Fink

In 1939, while out of town with their new musical TOO MANY GIRLS, Richard Rodgers and Lorenz Hart received a letter from writer John O'Hara. He asked if they would like to write a musical based on his series of *New Yorker* short stories about a fast-talking Chicago cad whose adventures were told in the form of letters signed "Pal Joey." The idea was provocative and, with an anti-hero at its heartless heart, a challenge to Rodgers & Hart. They quickly said yes. "Not only would the show be totally different from anything we had ever done before," noted Rodgers in his autobiography, *Musical Stages*, "it would be different from anything anyone else had ever tried."

Working closely with George Abbott, who had signed on as the musical's director and producer, O'Hara sculpted a narrative that was worldly-wise and steeped in sex. The central story revolved around Joey and his affair with a society dame, Vera Simpson; Vivienne Segal was cast as Vera (the character, created for the musical, shared Segal's initials) and the title role went to a talented young hoofer named Gene Kelly. The supporting cast included June Havoc, Van Johnson and Stanley Donen.

"Throughout our score for PAL JOEY," Rodgers recalled in his autobiography, "Larry and I were scrupulous in making every song adhere to the hard-edged nature of the story...Because of the night-club setting of most of the musical's action, [we] were able to have fun writing numbers burlesquing typically-tacky floor shows." The juxtaposition of plot songs alongside nightclub numbers was groundbreaking in 1940, and foreshadowed similar concepts used in such later musicals as GUYS AND DOLLS, CABARET and FOLLIES.

After a Philadelphia tryout, PAL JOEY opened at the Ethel Barrymore Theatre on Christmas night, 1940. Critical reaction was mixed; a few applauded the work's innovative sophistication and unflinching depiction of a "heel." But the prevailing critical response was summarized by this famous indictment from the *New York Times*: "Although it is expertly done, can you draw sweet water from a foul well?"

While far from a failure, PAL JOEY had a Broadway run of less than a year. Perhaps, like CHICAGO (another gin-and-jazz-soaked musical set in the Windy City that had to wait years for the public to catch up with it), PAL JOEY was ahead of its time. The score in particular seemed to spark surprisingly little interest; it too would have to wait for that spark to catch fire.

PAL JOEY's time was to come one decade later, and the impetus was the score's stand-out ballad, "Bewitched, Bothered and Bewildered." In the spring and summer of 1950, bandleaders and pop singers discovered the song; before long, seven versions had reached the top of the charts, with five of them making the Top 10. Capitalizing on this trend, in September of 1950, legendary Columbia Records President Goddard Lieberson produced a studio cast recording of the entire PAL JOEY score, teaming original star Segal with newcomer Harold Lang.

The album proved so popular that another look at the show was inevitable. Produced by Jule Styne, PAL JOEY came back to Broadway on January 3, 1952. Born in the twilight of the Rodgers & Hart musical comedy years, PAL JOEY returned 12 years later to a Broadway irrevocably altered by the Rodgers & Hammerstein revolution. Playing alongside SOUTH PACIFIC and THE KING AND I, Joey shared an audience primed for maturity and depth.

This time around, PAL JOEY was a hit. It featured the stars of the album, Segal and Lang, joined by Helen Gallagher (as Gladys) and Elaine Stritch (as the "Zip"-belting reporter). It outran the original by almost half a year, launched a 12-city national tour, and received the New York Drama Critics' Circle Award as Best Musical. A London production followed two years later, starring Lang and Carol Bruce.

The film version came out in 1957. Starring Frank Sinatra as Joey, with Rita Hayworth as Vera and Kim Novak as Linda (both ladies dubbed for their musical numbers), PAL JOEY on screen shifted the locale from Chicago to San Francisco, toned down the sex, threw out half the score and interpolated a host of other Rodgers & Hart standards. (Noted the *New Yorker*: "The score has been purified along with Joey's character...")

Its classic status assured, PAL JOEY has enjoyed many notable productions over the years, including two at New York's City Center: the first (in 1961) starring London's original Vera, Carol Bruce; the second (in 1963) with Viveca Lindfors, and both featuring the incomparable Bob Fosse in the title role. City Center was also home to a landmark concert version of PAL JOEY in 1995 as part of the celebrated series, *Encores! Great American Musicals in Concert*, starring Patti LuPone and Peter Gallagher.

Joey has danced his way back onto Broadway several times. A 1976 production at Circle in the Square starred Christopher Chadman, Joan Copeland and Dixie Carter, while a 2008 version, with a new script by Richard Greenberg, was presented by the Roundabout Theatre Company at Studio 54 and starred Stockard Channing, Matthew Risch and Martha Plimpton. Reviewing that production, the *Wall Street Journal* hailed PAL JOEY as "one of the best musicals of the 20th Century."

Cocky and confident, Joey Evans would have no doubt agreed.

A GREAT BIG TOWN
(Chicago)

Words by LORENZ HART
Music by RICHARD RODGERS

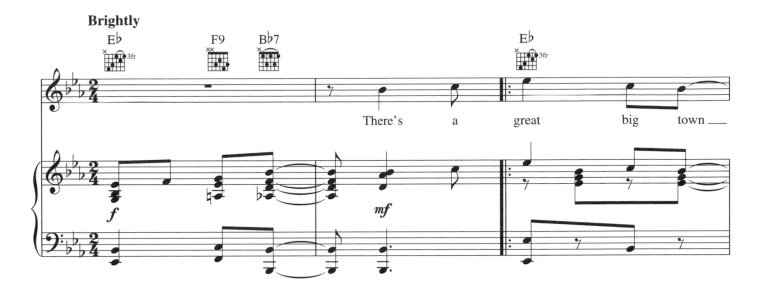

YOU MUSTN'T KICK IT AROUND

Words by LORENZ HART
Music by RICHARD RODGERS

I COULD WRITE A BOOK

Words by LORENZ HART
Music by RICHARD RODGERS

11

THAT TERRIFIC RAINBOW

Words by LORENZ HART
Music by RICHARD RODGERS

WHAT IS A MAN?

Words by LORENZ HART
Music by RICHARD RODGERS

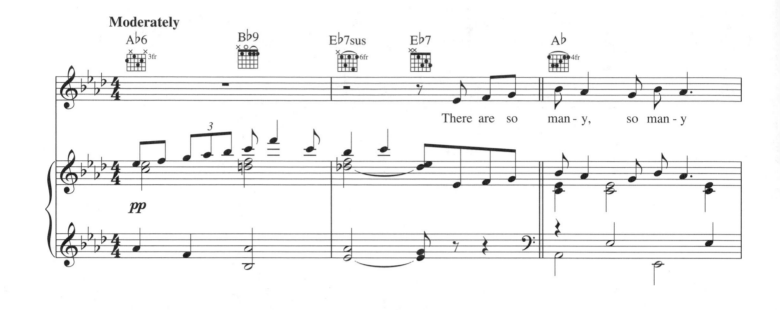

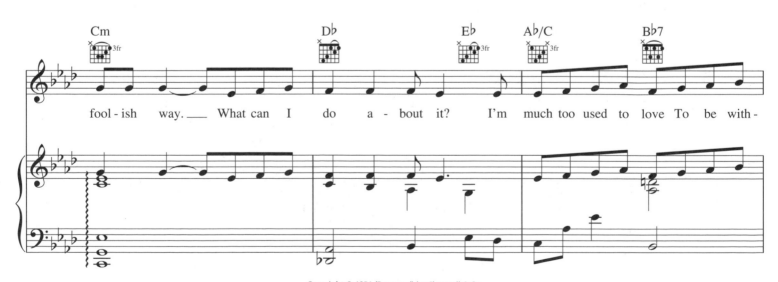

HAPPY HUNTING HORN

Words by LORENZ HART
Music by RICHARD RODGERS

BEWITCHED

Words by LORENZ HART
Music by RICHARD RODGERS

* *Standard lyric (in italics)*
** *Original show lyric.*

PAL JOEY
(What Do I Care for a Dame?)

Words by LORENZ HART
Music by RICHARD RODGERS

What do I care for a dame? _____

What do I care for a dame? _____

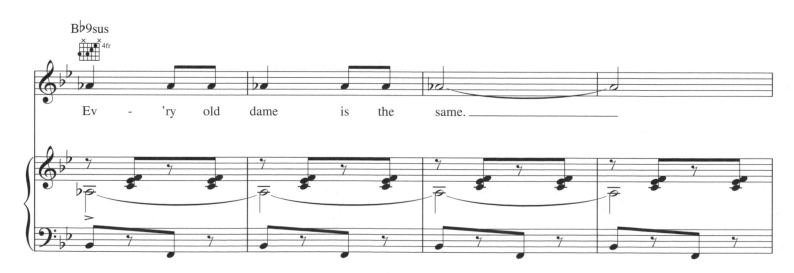

Ev-'ry old dame is the same. _____

THE FLOWER GARDEN OF MY HEART

Words by LORENZ HART
Music by RICHARD RODGERS

DEN OF INIQUITY

Words by LORENZ HART
Music By RICHARD RODGERS

Just two lit-tle love-birds all a-lone In a lit-tle co-zy nest

With a lit-tle se-cret tel-e-phone; That's the place to rest.

Ar-ti-fi-cial ros-es round the door— They are nev-er out of bloom—

47

ZIP

Words by LORENZ HART
Music by RICHARD RODGERS

Moderately

I've in-ter-viewed Pa-blo Pi-cas-so And a

count-ess named di Fras-so. I've in-ter-viewed the great Stra-vin-sky. But my

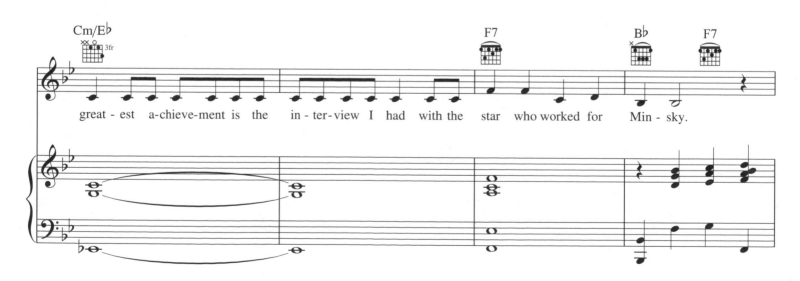

great-est a-chieve-ment is the in-ter-view I had with the star who worked for Min-sky.

50

DO IT THE HARD WAY

Words by LORENZ HART
Music by RICHARD RODGERS

TAKE HIM

Words by LORENZ HART
Music by RICHARD RODGERS

He was a cut-ie— I ad-mit I used to care.
Thanks lit-tle mous-ey for the pres-ent and all that,

But it's my du-ty to my-self to take the air.
But in this hous-ey, I would rath-er keep a rat.

I won't pre-vent you from e-lop-ing if you wish.
On-ly a wiz-ard could re-form that class of males.

I'M TALKING TO MY PAL

Words by LORENZ HART
Music by RICHARD RODGERS